Fish Facts

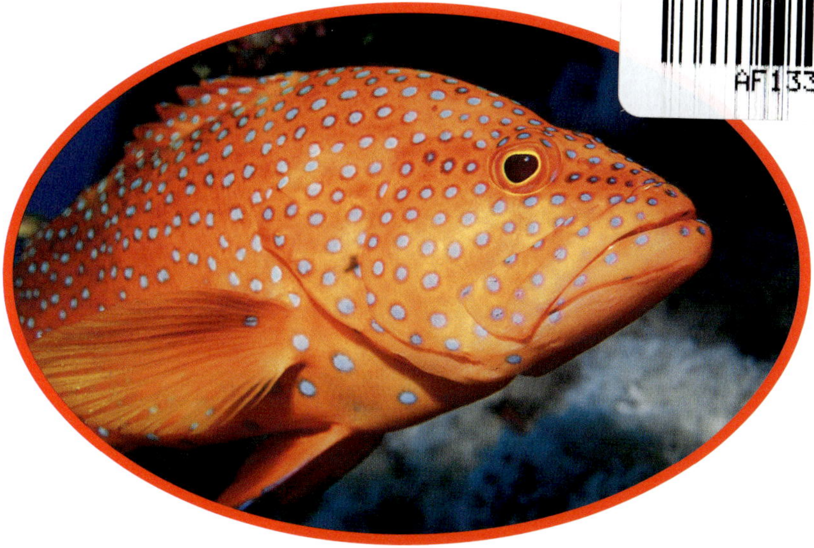

Alison Hawes

RIGBY

Fish live in water.

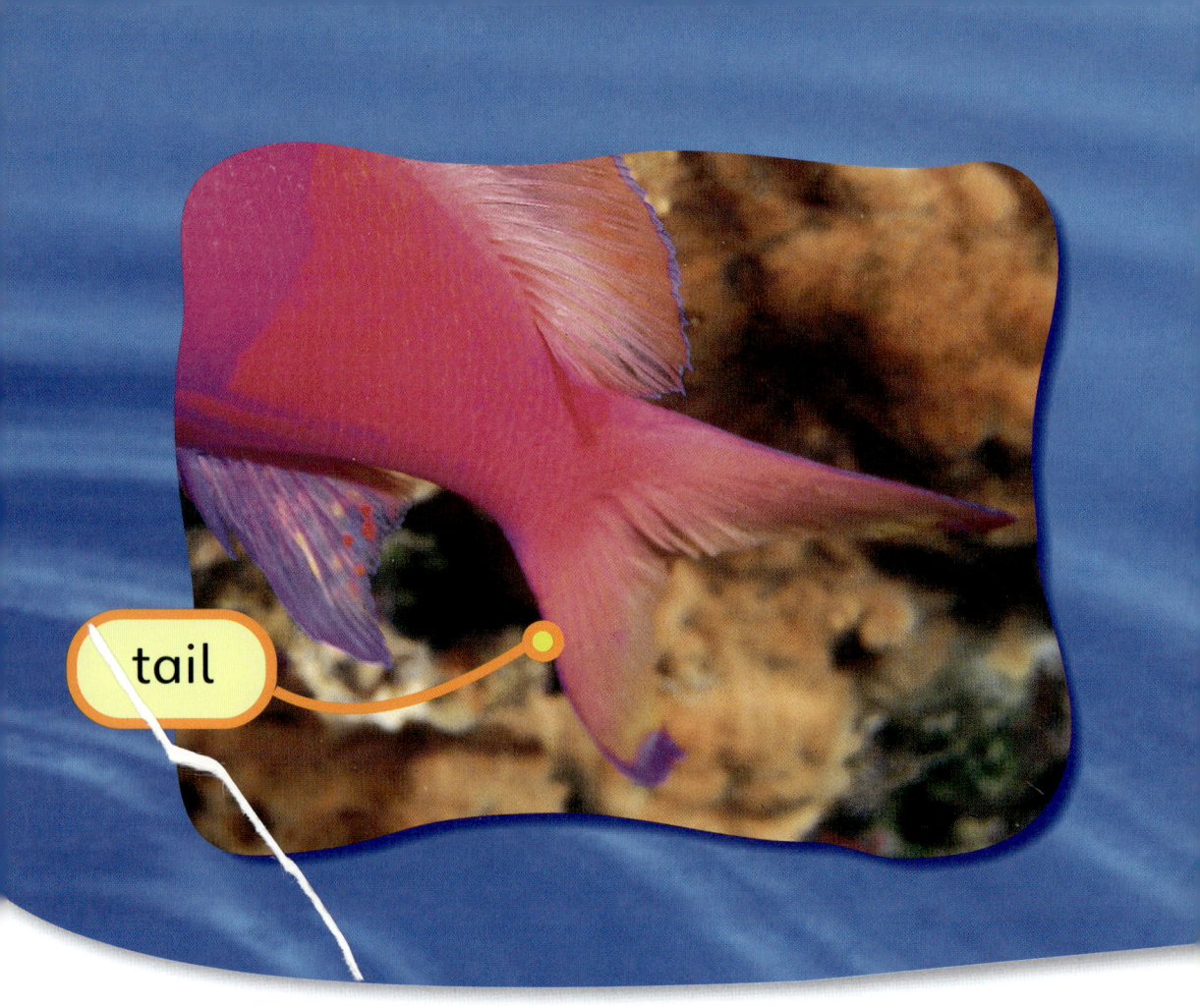

Fish have a tail.

Look at the tail on this fish.

Fish have gills.

Look at the gills on this fish.

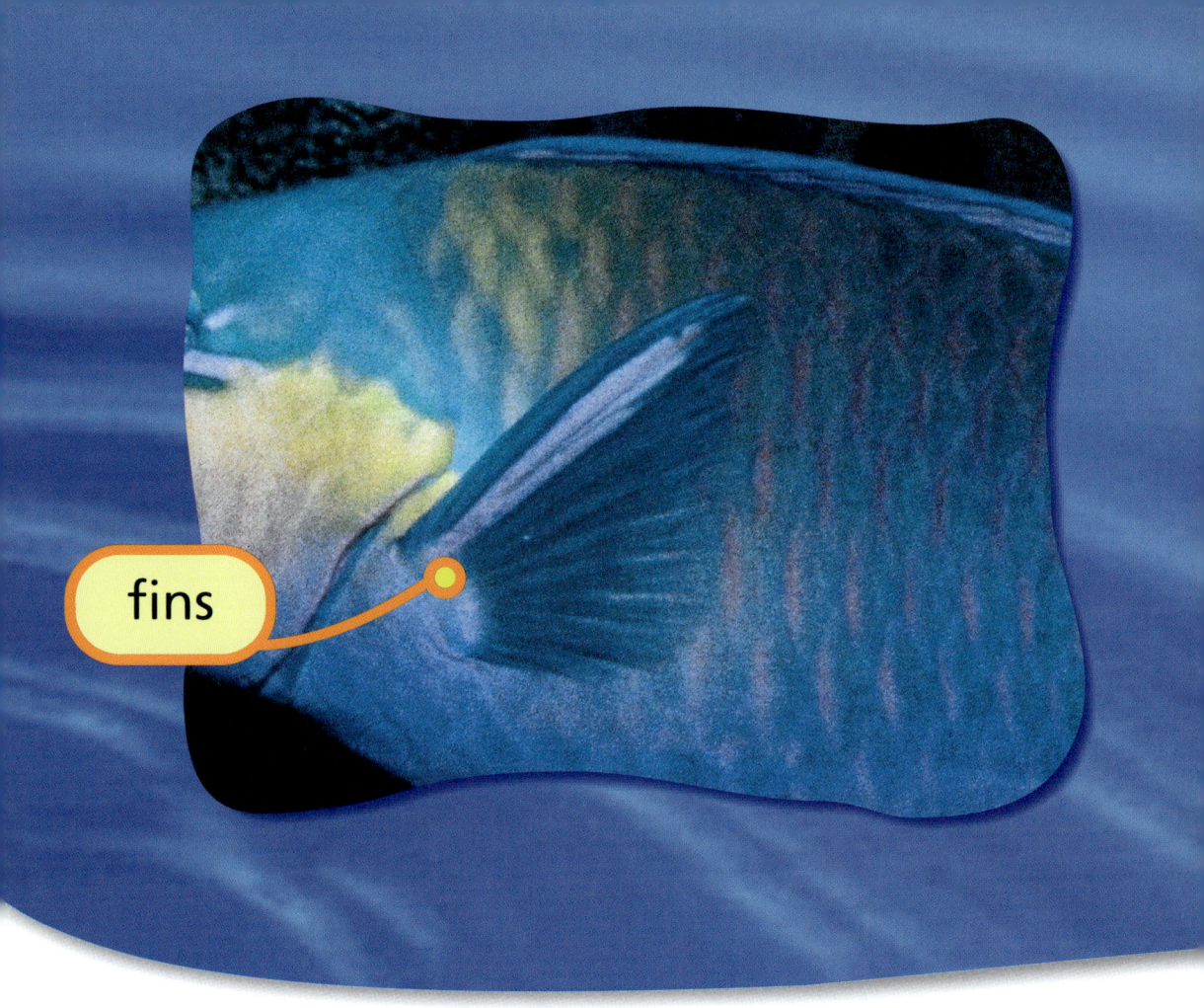

Fish have fins.

Look at the fins on this fish.

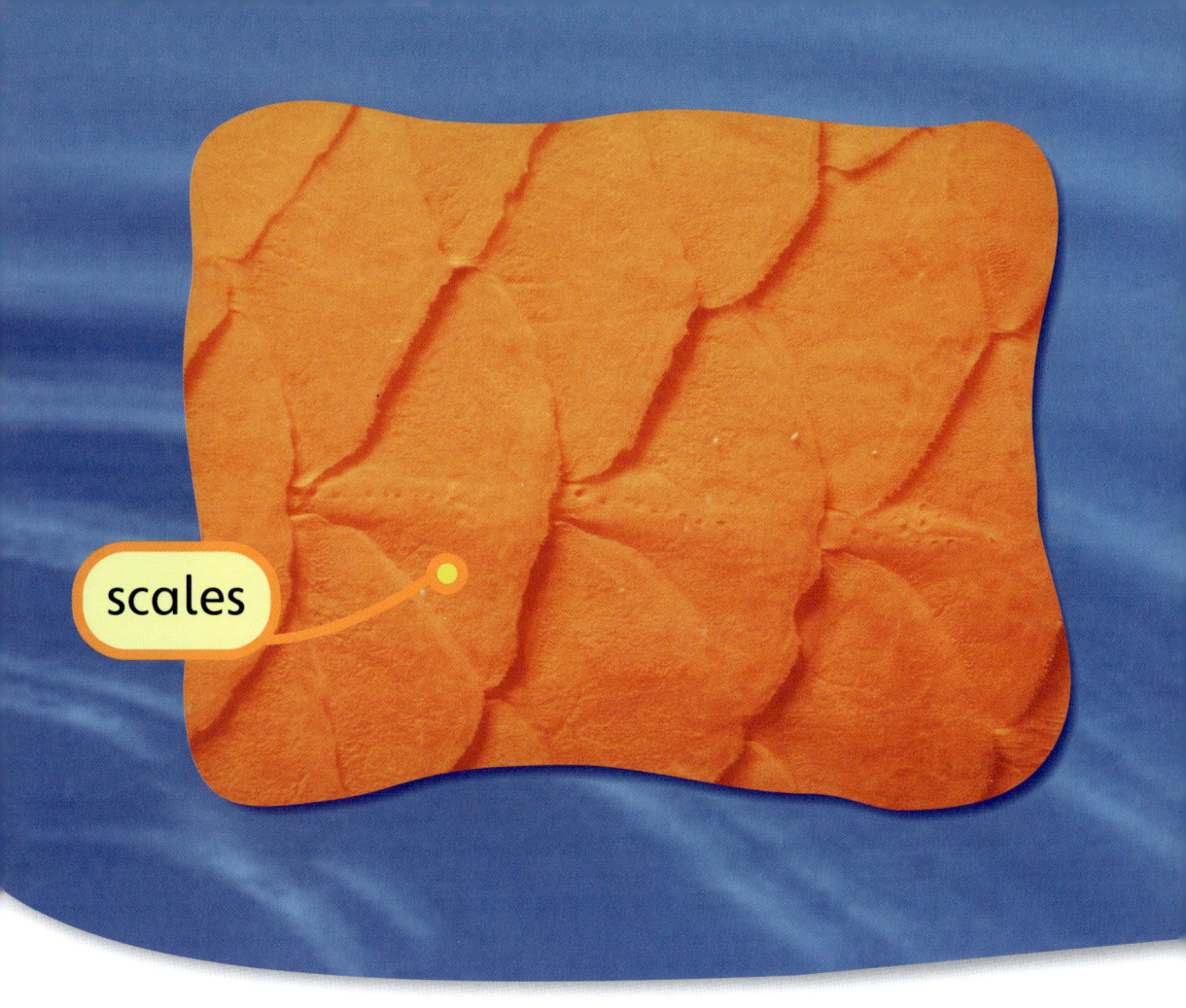

Fish have scales.

Look at the scales on this fish.

Fish have a tail and gills and fins and scales.